Potluck

by
Linda Kita-Bradley

Grass Roots Press

Potluck is published by
Grass Roots Press, a division of Literacy Services of Canada Ltd.

www.grassrootsbooks.net

ACKNOWLEDGMENTS

We acknowledge the financial support of the Government of Canada through the Canada Book Fund (CBF) for our publishing activities.

Produced with the assistance of the Government of Alberta, Alberta Multimedia Development Fund.

**Government
of Alberta ■**

Editor: Dr. Pat Campbell
Photography: Grass Roots Press
Book design: Lara Minja, Lime Design Inc.

Library and Archives Canada Cataloguing in Publication

Kita-Bradley, Linda, 1958–
    Potluck / Linda Kita-Bradley.

ISBN 978–1–926583–90–7

    1. Readers for new literates. 2. Readers—Ethics. I. Title.

PE1126.N43K5865 2012   428.6'2   C2012–903011–2

This is Mel.

Mel is going to a potluck dinner.

Mel wants to make beef stew.

Mel has potatoes.

He has onions.

He has carrots.

He has beef.

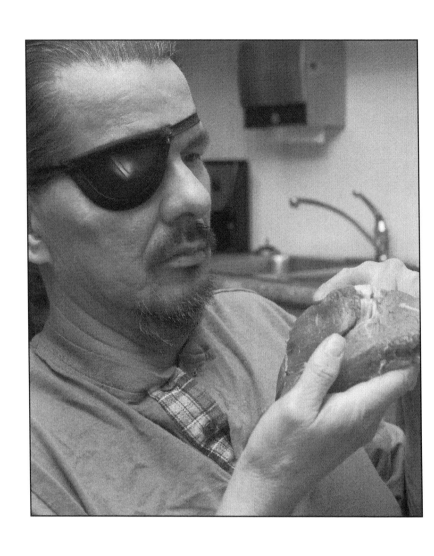

A part of the beef looks bad.

Mel cuts off the bad part.

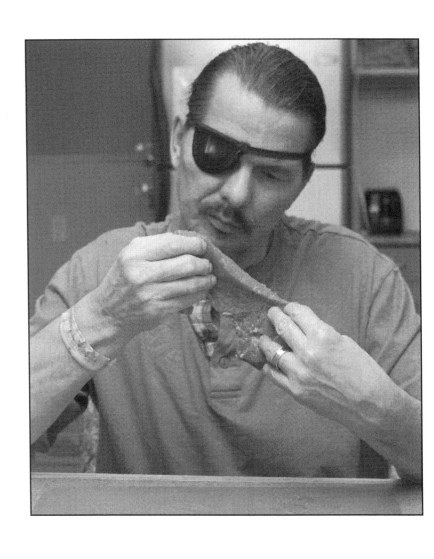

Mel thinks, "Is this beef safe?"

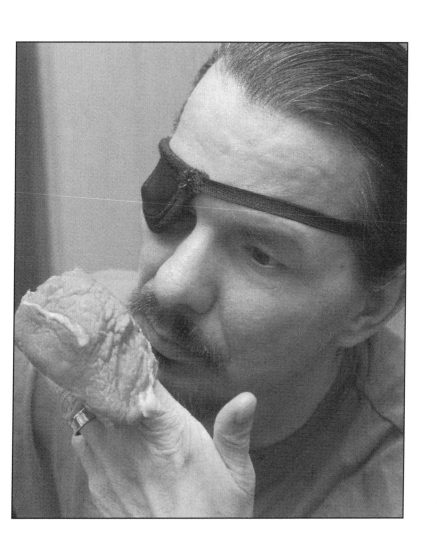

The beef smells okay.

Mel puts the beef in the pot.

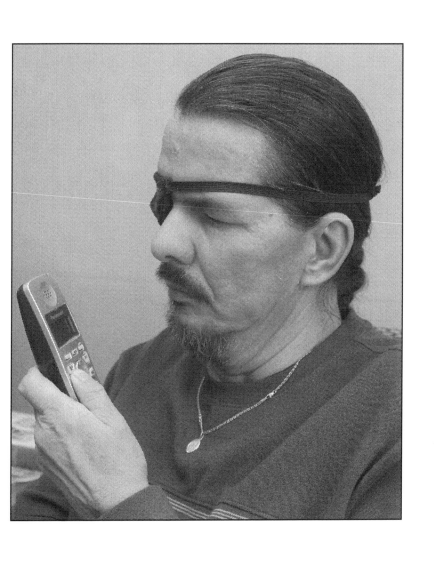

Mel gets a call the next day.

Mel says, "Hi, Pam."

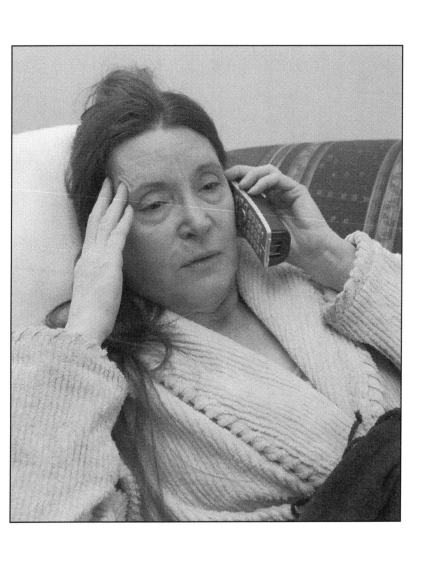

Pam says, "I am so sick."

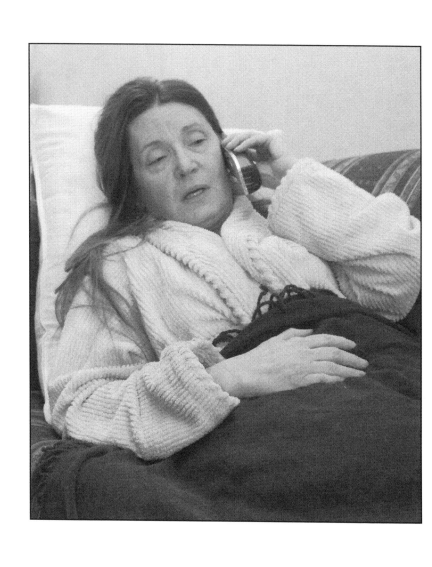

"I think I ate some bad food."

Mel thinks about the beef.

He cut off the bad part.

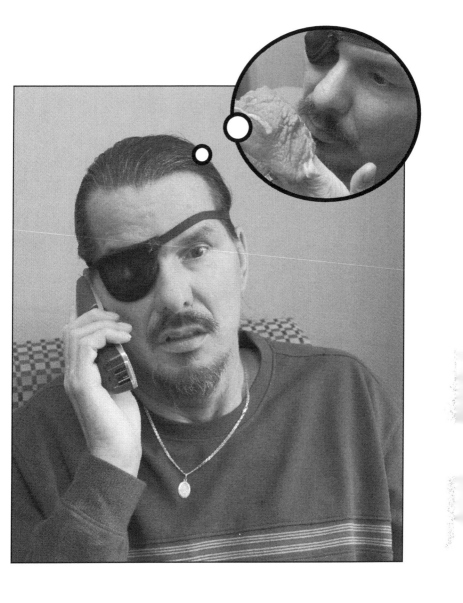

The beef smelled okay.

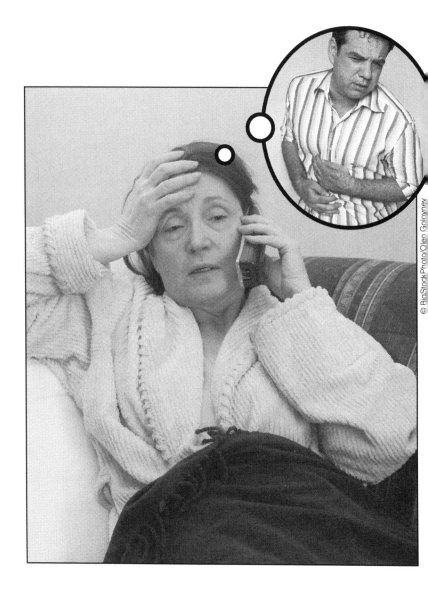

Pam says, "Ron is sick, too."

"We think the fish was bad."

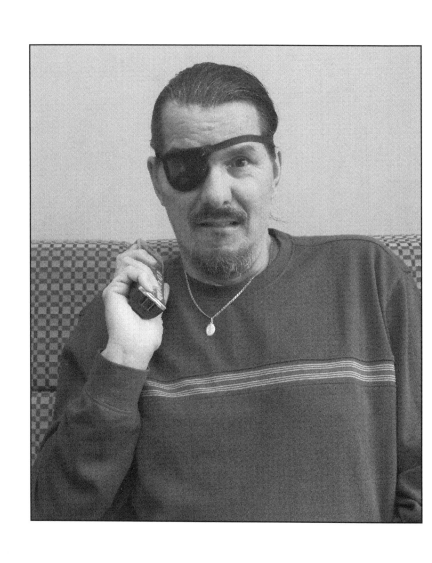

Should Mel tell Pam
about the beef?

■

Made in United States
Troutdale, OR
02/28/2024

18060316R00015